STRONGHOLD
Journal Your Journey

Remade

REMADE MINISTRIES
VACAVILLE, CALIFORNIA, USA

Remade
FREE. KNOWN. HEARD.

Copyright 2015 © Beth Kinder

Published by Remade Ministries

Vacaville, CA 95687

remadecommunity.org

bethkinder.com

All Scripture quotations are from the New Living Translation unless otherwise stated.

Edited by Laura Davis

Cover Design Jen Ybarra

All rights reserved. This book or parts thereof may not be reproduced in any form, except for brief quotations in reviews without written permission from the publisher.

Printed in the United States of America

ISBN-13:978-1530286294

ISBN-10:1530286298

TABLE *of* CONTENTS

Introduction 6

Chapter 1: The Stronghold 10

Chapter 2: A Friend For the Journey 24

Chapter 3: He Loves Me, He Loves Me Not 50

Chapter 4: Take Captive Those Thoughts 64

Chapter 5: Bondage of Busyness 80

Chapter 6: Trust His Name 108

Chapter 7: We Have Overcome 122

Journal Your Journey
INTRODUCTION

Prepare yourself for the journey of a lifetime, because you are being positioned to encounter the presence of God in your personal quiet time.

In the Old Testament before the Israelites crossed the Jordan River into their Promised Land, the Lord told Joshua to take 12 stones from the middle of the very waters that were separating them from their freedom. The people were to erect a memorial with these large boulders. The Lord explained to Joshua that these stones would cause people to ask what they were, and give opportunity to tell future generations how the God of Israel delivered them from captivity into their Promised Land. The Lord called these stones, Stones of Remembrance. (Joshua 4)

Your journal will become your personal stones of remembrance. When people ask what this is, you'll be able to share with them the journey God took you on from captivity to freedom.

You will record stories, moments from your past, and intimate encounters you have with God. One day you'll look back on these pages, and they will describe a fierce warrior who faced the unknown and let go of the chains from the past. This journal will represent the authentic stronghold you'll come to know.

It takes courage to look at the past, and boldness to break free from it. I assure you God is setting you up for success. He will loose what has kept you bound not just for your benefit, but also for the benefit of another.

Today is your day to leave the lies behind and walk into the truth of what God says about you and has promised for you.

The journal is designed to be a companion to the book. The questions in the book are conveniently provided throughout the journal along with ample space to record your conversations with God.

Enjoy your journey; it's the best part of the story.

Beth

The Lord is good, a stronghold when trouble comes.

He is close to those who trust in him

NAH. 1:7 (ESV)

CHAPTER 1

THE STRONGHOLD

— Journal Your Journey —

- Take time to ask the Lord what the counterfeit strongholds are in your life. Write in your journal the first words that come to your mind. You may have more than one counterfeit stronghold.
- Look up in the dictionary the definition of the words you've written down.
- Write down any revelations their definitions bring to you.

_____

_____

_____

_____

_____

_____

_____

_____

The Stronghold

"The Lord Almighty is with us; the God of Jacob is our fortress."

PSALM 46:11

Stronghold — The secrets beyond the wall

> " I will give you a new heart and put a new spirit in you; I will remove from you your heart of stone and give you a heart of flesh."
>
> EZEKIEL 36:26

The Stronghold

> "The Lord Almighty is with us; the God of Jacob is our fortress."
>
> PSALM 46:11

Stronghold — The secrets beyond the wall

Journal Your Journey

- Write Exodus 14:14 in the journal.
- Write in the journal any revelations from the Lord.

Stronghold — The secrets beyond the wall

> *"I will give you a new heart and put a new spirit in you; I will remove from you your heart of stone and give you a heart of flesh."*
>
> EZEKIEL 36:26

Journal Your Journey

- Write out what your default response is during a battle.
- Write out why you feel it is difficult to remain calm in battle.
- Next to your default responses write how God would call you to respond.
- Look up Ephesians 6:13–17. Write out verse 17 and underline the weapons listed in that verse.

Stronghold — The secrets beyond the wall

The Stronghold

> *"The Lord Almighty is with us; the God of Jacob is our fortress."*
>
> PSALM 46:11

Stronghold — The secrets beyond the wall

> " I will give you a new heart and put a new spirit in you; I will remove from you your heart of stone and give you a heart of flesh."
>
> EZEKIEL 36:26

The Stronghold

Stronghold — The secrets beyond the wall

It is not by force or by strength, but by my Spirit,

says the Lord of Heaven's Armies.

ZECHARIAH 4:6

CHAPTER 2

A FRIEND FOR THE JOURNEY

— *Journal Your Journey* —

- List some of the roads you keep returning to.
- Be honest before God and write about your fear of failing.

_____

_____

_____

_____

_____

_____

_____

_____

_____

_____

A Friend for the Journey

Sin is no longer your master, for you no longer live under the requirements of the law. Instead, you live under the freedom of God's grace.

ROMANS 6:14

Stronghold — The secrets beyond the wall

> *But now you are free from the power of sin and have become slaves of God. Now you do those things that lead to holiness and result in eternal life.*
>
> ROMANS 6:22

A Friend for the Journey

Sin is no longer your master, for you no longer live under the requirements of the law. Instead, you live under the freedom of God's grace.

ROMANS 6:14

Stronghold — The secrets beyond the wall

> *But now you are free from the power of sin and have become slaves of God. Now you do those things that lead to holiness and result in eternal life.*
>
> ROMANS 6:22

Journal Your Journey

- Let's pause and look up in our Bible Romans 6:6–7.
- Read the scripture and write down what it means to you in your journal.
- In light of these verses, journal your thoughts about the road you described earlier.

_____

_____

_____

_____

_____

_____

_____

_____

_____

_____

_____

_____

_____

_____

_____

_____

Stronghold — The secrets beyond the wall

A Friend for the Journey

Sin is no longer your master, for you no longer live under the requirements of the law. Instead, you live under the freedom of God's grace.

ROMANS 6:14

Stronghold — The secrets beyond the wall

But now you are free from the power of sin and have become slaves of God. Now you do those things that lead to holiness and result in eternal life.

ROMANS 6:22

Journal Your Journey

- Keeping in mind the difference between conviction and condemnation, write out which one you've been listening to and record your insights.
- Ask the Lord to reveal His truth to you.

Stronghold — The secrets beyond the wall

A Friend for the Journey

> *Sin is no longer your master, for you no longer live under the requirements of the law. Instead, you live under the freedom of God's grace.*
>
> ROMANS 6:14

Stronghold — The secrets beyond the wall

> *But now you are free from the power of sin and have become slaves of God. Now you do those things that lead to holiness and result in eternal life.*
>
> ROMANS 6:22

Journal Your Journey

- Write what type of relationship you feel you have with the Holy Spirit —unknown, distant, personal.
- Write a prayer telling Him the type of relationship you desire to have with Him.
- Ask Him for a strategy to help you develop it.

Stronghold — The secrets beyond the wall

A Friend for the Journey

> *Sin is no longer your master, for you no longer live under the requirements of the law. Instead, you live under the freedom of God's grace.*
>
> ROMANS 6:14

Stronghold — The secrets beyond the wall

> *But now you are free from the power of sin and have become slaves of God. Now you do those things that lead to holiness and result in eternal life.*
>
> ROMANS 6:22

A Friend for the Journey

Sin is no longer your master, for you no longer live under the requirements of the law. Instead, you live under the freedom of God's grace.

ROMANS 6:14

Stronghold — The secrets beyond the wall

> *But now you are free from the power of sin and have become slaves of God. Now you do those things that lead to holiness and result in eternal life.*
>
> ROMANS 6:22

Journal Your Journey

In your Bible look up and read Romans 8:31–39, answering the following questions:

- Who can be against us? (Rom. 8:31)
- Did God spare anything for us? (Rom. 8:32)
- Will God give everything to us? (Rom. 8:32)
- Why can't charges be brought against us? (Rom. 8:33-34)
- What are we called? (Rom. 8:37)
- Can anything ever separate us from Christ's love? (Rom. 8:39)

Stronghold — The secrets beyond the wall

A Friend for the Journey

> *Sin is no longer your master, for you no longer live under the requirements of the law. Instead, you live under the freedom of God's grace.*
>
> ROMANS 6:14

Stronghold — The secrets beyond the wall

> *But now you are free from the power of sin and have become slaves of God. Now you do those things that lead to holiness and result in eternal life.*
>
> ROMANS 6:22

A Friend for the Journey

Stronghold — The secrets beyond the wall

We know how much God loves us and we put our trust in His love. God is love, and all who live in love live in God, and God lives in them.

1 JOHN 4:16

CHAPTER 3

HE LOVES ME, HE LOVES ME NOT

Journal Your Journey

- Take a moment to write down how you view the character of God.
- Do you think of a loving God when you think of God?
- What type of person do you think God would love?

He Loves Me, He Loves Me Not

Journal Your Journey

- Describe in your own words what you think love is.

He Loves Me, He Loves Me Not

And I am convinced that nothing can ever separate us from God's love. Neither death nor life, neither angels nor demons, neither our fears for today nor our worries about tomorrow—not even the powers of hell can separate us from God's love.

ROMANS 8:38

Stronghold — The secrets beyond the wall

But anyone who does not love does not know God, for God is love.

1 JOHN 4:8

Journal Your Journey

- Take a moment to list those who have marked your heart and spoken over your life that you were not worth it.

- Write out who they were and what they did, then go down that list one by one and say: "I am worth loving. I forgive you."

- Dear friend, don't wrestle with forgiving them. Your forgiveness is not saying what they did was right. Your forgiveness is unlocking your prison door.

Stronghold — The secrets beyond the wall

He Loves Me, He Loves Me Not

And I am convinced that nothing can ever separate us from God's love. Neither death nor life, neither angels nor demons, neither our fears for today nor our worries about tomorrow—not even the powers of hell can separate us from God's love.

ROMANS 8:38

Stronghold — The secrets beyond the wall

> *But anyone who does not love does not know God, for God is love.*
>
> 1 JOHN 4:8

Journal Your Journey

P.S. An after thought . . .

- Go back in your journal where you wrote what loves means to you. Is there anything you'd like to change about that?
- Then go back to our key scripture, and write what speaks to you about that scripture in light of knowing who God is.

Stronghold — The secrets beyond the wall

He Loves Me, He Loves Me Not

Stronghold — The secrets beyond the wall

I prayed to the LORD, and he answered me.

He freed me from all my fears.

PSALM 34:4

CHAPTER 4

TAKE CAPTIVE THOSE THOUGHTS
Journal Your Journey

- Take a moment and ask the Lord to reveal to you the "suddenlies" in your life that have altered the landscape of your mind.

_____

_____

_____

_____

_____

_____

_____

_____

_____

_____

Take Captive Those Thoughts

*The Lord is my rock, my
fortress and my deliverer;
my God is my rock,
in whom I take refuge,
my shield and the horn
of my salvation,
my stronghold.*

PSALM 18:2 (NIV)

Stronghold — The secrets beyond the wall

> We destroy every proud obstacle that keeps people from knowing God. We capture their rebellious thoughts and teach them to obey Christ.
>
> 2 CORINTHIANS 10:5

Journal Your Journey

- List in your journal some of the thoughts you may have aligned with and look up the scripture.
- Write out the scriptures that are truth against the lies you've believed.
- Choose the one that stands out the most and record it on either a 3x5 card, sticky note, or the home screen of your phone.
- Place the card or sticky note in a place you frequent in order to meditate on that scripture.

Stronghold — The secrets beyond the wall

Take Captive Those Thoughts

The Lord is my rock, my fortress and my deliverer; my God is my rock, in whom I take refuge, my shield and the horn of my salvation, my stronghold.

PSALM 18:2 (NIV)

Stronghold — The secrets beyond the wall

> *We destroy every proud obstacle that keeps people from knowing God. We capture their rebellious thoughts and teach them to obey Christ.*
>
> 2 CORINTHIANS 10:5

Journal Your Journey

Read Genesis 2:16–18 and 3:1–13 in your Bible.

Answer the following:

- What was the command for the trees? (Genesis 2:16–17)
- Was Eve there when the command was given? (Genesis 2:18)
- How is the serpent described? (Genesis 3:1)
- Did Eve recognize the first lie the serpent told? (Genesis 3:2)
- Did Eve quote God's command correctly back to the enemy? (Genesis 3:3)
- Did Eve recognize the second lie the serpent told? (Genesis 3:6)
- What did Eve confess to the Lord? (Genesis 3:13)

_____

_____

_____

_____

_____

_____

_____

_____

Stronghold — The secrets beyond the wall

Take Captive Those Thoughts

The Lord is my rock, my fortress and my deliverer; my God is my rock, in whom I take refuge, my shield and the horn of my salvation, my stronghold.

PSALM 18:2 (NIV)

Stronghold — The secrets beyond the wall

> We destroy every proud obstacle that keeps people from knowing God. We capture their rebellious thoughts and teach them to obey Christ.
>
> 2 CORINTHIANS 10:5

Journal Your Journey

- Write in your journal the top three lies you have believed.
- As you spend time in His presence this week, consider the lies and ask for scriptural truths to defeat them.
- Commit to being a firsthand consumer of the word of God.

Stronghold — The secrets beyond the wall

Take Captive Those Thoughts

Stronghold — The secrets beyond the wall

He who dwells in the shelter of the Most High, will rest in the shadow of the Almighty.

PSALM 91:1

CHAPTER 5

BONDAGE OF BUSYNESS

— Journal Your Journey —

- In your journal, list God's order.
- Next list the order of your life.
- Compare the two and write out a prayer asking for wisdom and a strategy to align the two.

_____
_____
_____
_____
_____
_____
_____
_____
_____

Bondage of Busyness

> *But he said to me, "My grace is sufficient for you, for my power is made perfect in weakness." Therefore I will boast all the more gladly about my weaknesses, so that Christ's power may rest on me.*
>
> 2 CORINTHIANS 12:9 (NIV)

Stronghold — The secrets beyond the wall

> *Pay careful attention to your own work, for then you will get the satisfaction of a job well done, and you won't need to compare yourself to anyone else.*
>
> GALATIANS 6:4

Journal Your Journey

Choose one type of prayer and focus for 5–10 minutes. Journal about your experience after you are finished.

- What feelings did you experience toward God?
- What are some of the discoveries you made while in prayer?
- How did the presence of God feel?
- Were there any challenges during your focused time?

Stronghold — The secrets beyond the wall

Bondage of Busyness

But he said to me, "My grace is sufficient for you, for my power is made perfect in weakness." Therefore I will boast all the more gladly about my weaknesses, so that Christ's power may rest on me.

2 CORINTHIANS 12:9 (NIV)

Stronghold — The secrets beyond the wall

*Pay careful attention to
your own work,
for then you will get the
satisfaction of a job well
done, and you won't need
to compare yourself to
anyone else.*

GALATIANS 6:4

Journal Your Journey

Choose one type of worship and focus for 5–10 minutes. Journal about your experience after you are finished.

- What feelings did you experience toward God?
- What are some of the discoveries you made while in worship?
- How did the presence of God feel?
- Were there any challenges during your focused time?

Stronghold — The secrets beyond the wall

Bondage of Busyness

> *But he said to me, "My grace is sufficient for you, for my power is made perfect in weakness." Therefore I will boast all the more gladly about my weaknesses, so that Christ's power may rest on me.*
>
> 2 CORINTHIANS 12:9 (NIV)

Stronghold — The secrets beyond the wall

Pay careful attention to your own work, for then you will get the satisfaction of a job well done, and you won't need to compare yourself to anyone else.

GALATIANS 6:4

Journal Your Journey

Focus for 5–10 minutes on studying one verse. Journal about your experience after you are finished.

- What feelings did you experience toward God?
- What are some of the discoveries you made while in study?
- How did the presence of God feel?
- Were there any challenges during your focused time?

Stronghold — The secrets beyond the wall

Bondage of Busyness

> *But he said to me, "My grace is sufficient for you, for my power is made perfect in weakness." Therefore I will boast all the more gladly about my weaknesses, so that Christ's power may rest on me.*
>
> 2 CORINTHIANS 12:9 (NIV)

Stronghold — The secrets beyond the wall

Pay careful attention to your own work, for then you will get the satisfaction of a job well done, and you won't need to compare yourself to anyone else.

GALATIANS 6:4

Journal Your Journey

- Are you caught in a comparison trap?
- Take time to journal about what you are comparing yourself to, and why you think you do this.
- What fear-based absolutes are you listening to?
- Write out some faith-filled declarations in response to them.

Stronghold — The secrets beyond the wall

Bondage of Busyness

> *But he said to me, "My grace is sufficient for you, for my power is made perfect in weakness." Therefore I will boast all the more gladly about my weaknesses, so that Christ's power may rest on me.*
>
> 2 CORINTHIANS 12:9 (NIV)

Stronghold — The secrets beyond the wall

Pay careful attention to your own work, for then you will get the satisfaction of a job well done, and you won't need to compare yourself to anyone else.

GALATIANS 6:4

Journal Your Journey

- List in your journal the opportunities that have become your responsibilities.
- Write out any "I am afraid if…" responses to any of these responsibilities.
- Write out how the Lord would have you respond to those responsibilities.

Stronghold — The secrets beyond the wall

Bondage of Busyness

But he said to me, "My grace is sufficient for you, for my power is made perfect in weakness." Therefore I will boast all the more gladly about my weaknesses, so that Christ's power may rest on me.

2 CORINTHIANS 12:9 (NIV)

Stronghold — The secrets beyond the wall

> *Pay careful attention to your own work, for then you will get the satisfaction of a job well done, and you won't need to compare yourself to anyone else.*
>
> GALATIANS 6:4

Journal Your Journey

- List the longings you have in your heart.
- Write out a prayer surrendering those dreams and hopes.
- Commit in prayer to releasing your busy life and embracing a life of rest.

Stronghold — The secrets beyond the wall

Bondage of Busyness

Stronghold — The secrets beyond the wall

Those who know your name trust in you, for you O Lord, do not abandon those who search for you.

PSALM 9:10

CHAPTER 6
TRUST HIS NAME
— Journal Your Journey —

- Draw an altar on the pages of your notebook.
- Write above the altar what or who hurt you.
- Record a prayer asking God to reveal His character at this altar.

Trust His Name

> *Search me, God,
> and know my heart;
> test me and know my
> anxious thoughts.*
>
> PSALM 139:23

Stronghold — The secrets beyond the wall

> *I will give them a heart to know Me, for I am the Lord; and they will be My people, and I will be their God, for they will return to Me with their whole heart.*
>
> JEREMIAH 24:7 NASB

Journal Your Journey

Here is your woman at the well moment. Jesus has come to give you freedom and purpose through it.

- Ask the Lord what He wants to do with your pain.
- Ask Him how you should respond to the pain.
- Ask Him how He will use it for His glory.
- Journal all He reveals to you.

Stronghold — The secrets beyond the wall

Trust His Name

> *Search me, God,
> and know my heart;
> test me and know my
> anxious thoughts.*
>
> PSALM 139:23

Stronghold — The secrets beyond the wall

I will give them a heart to know Me, for I am the Lord; and they will be My people, and I will be their God, for they will return to Me with their whole heart.

JEREMIAH 24:7 NASB

Journal Your Journey

You have been invited to enter into the chambers.

- Visualize what that looks like.
- Mentally approach His throne.
- Imagine laying the offerings upon the altar.
- Confess out loud what you are offering there.
- Declare you no longer own them.
- Record the experience in your journal.

Stronghold — The secrets beyond the wall

Trust His Name

> *Search me, God, and know my heart; test me and know my anxious thoughts.*
>
> PSALM 139:23

Stronghold — The secrets beyond the wall

I will give them a heart to know Me, for I am the Lord; and they will be My people, and I will be their God, for they will return to Me with their whole heart.

JEREMIAH 24:7 NASB

Trust His Name

Stronghold — The secrets beyond the wall

They overcame him by the blood of the lamb and the word of their testimony; they did not love their lives somuch as to shrink from death.

REV. 12:11 (NIV)

CHAPTER 7

WE HAVE OVERCOME

Journal Your Journey

- Pray that God would connect you to the one ahead of you.
- Now pray to be connected to the one behind you.
- Ask the Lord what He wants you to do with your story.
- Journal what you sense the Spirit is saying.

_____

_____

_____

_____

_____

_____

_____

_____

_____

We Have Overcome

> *But we all, with unveiled face, beholding as in a mirror the glory of the Lord, are being transformed into the same image from glory to glory, just as from the Lord, the Spirit.*
>
> 2 CORINTHIANS 3:18 NASB

Stronghold — The secrets beyond the wall

For we are not fighting against flesh-and-blood enemies, but against evil rulers and authorities of the unseen world, against mighty powers in this dark world, and against evil spirits in the heavenly places.

EPHESIANS 6:12

We Have Overcome

But we all, with unveiled face, beholding as in a mirror the glory of the Lord, are being transformed into the same image from glory to glory, just as from the Lord, the Spirit.

2 CORINTHIANS 3:18 NASB

Stronghold — The secrets beyond the wall

> For we are not fighting against flesh-and-blood enemies, but against evil rulers and authorities of the unseen world, against mighty powers in this dark world, and against evil spirits in the heavenly places.
>
> EPHESIANS 6:12

We Have Overcome

Stronghold — The secrets beyond the wall

Remade
RESOURCES

STRONGHOLDTHEBOOK.COM
Stronghold Video Series
Stronghold Study Group Questions
Scripture Memory Cards

REMADECOMMUNITY.ORG
Walk Through Ephesians A 20-day Journey Bible Study
Faith Over Fear Video Series

BETHKINDER.COM

ONLINE BIBLICAL RESOURCES
BIBLEHUB.COM
BIBLEGATEWAY.COM

NATIONAL SEXUAL ASSAULT HOTLINE
800.656.HOPE (4673)
RAINN.ORG

Made in the USA
Charleston, SC
05 April 2016